Crescendo

Voices of the Waves

Sara Samuel

BookLeaf Publishing

India | USA | UK

Dedication

For my Father,

Whose love has been the steady rhythm steering my life.

With every rising moment, building like a crescendo, it is your wisdom, patience, and strength that reverberate through these pages.

This collection of poems is a tribute to the lessons you have instilled and the dreams you have nurtured, reaching their peak in the symphony of my words.

May these poems reflect the depth of your influence and the crescendo of my gratitude.

With all my love,

Sara

Acknowledgement

This collection, *Crescendo: Voices of the Waves*, would not have come to life without the unwavering support and encouragement of many wonderful individuals.

First and foremost, I extend my deepest gratitude to my family , whose constant love, support, and wisdom have been a beacon throughout my life as well as my creative journey. Their belief in me has been the driving force behind every word on these pages.

To my friends and loved ones, your encouragement and patience have been invaluable. Your presence and feedback have shaped this work in ways I am deeply grateful for.

Finally, to every reader who picks up this book, thank you for your time and openness. I hope these poems resonate with you and reflect the ebb and flow of our shared emotional experiences.

With heartfelt gratitude,
Sara

Preface

In the quiet moments of daily life, where routine intertwines with reflection, we often find ourselves swept away by a symphony of emotions. This collection, *Crescendo: Voices of the Waves*, seeks to capture those subtle yet profound feelings that rise and fall with the rhythms of our everyday existence.

Each poem in this book is an exploration of the emotional crescendo that builds within us, the silent peaks and valleys of life's experiences. Just as a symphony is crafted by its varied movements, so too are our lives composed of myriad emotions, each contributing to the greater harmony of our personal stories.

This work is inspired by the simple, yet powerful moments that define us, and it is dedicated to my loved ones and friends whose steadfast support and wisdom have been a guiding force. Their influence resonates throughout these pages, as the enduring strength behind my words.

I invite you to immerse yourself in these verses, to discover reflections of your own experiences, and to recognize the beauty in the everyday symphony of our lives. May these poems resonate with you as they have with me, capturing the essence of our shared human experiences.

.

Thank you for joining me on this journey.
Sara

Glimmer of Love

In the hush of night, where shadows play,
A glimmer of love finds its gentle way.
Through whispered winds and starry skies,
It softly dances in lovers' eyes.

A fleeting glance, a tender smile,
A moment's touch that lingers awhile.
In the quiet hum of hearts that beat,
The glimmer of love feels so sweet.

It's in the blush of dawn's first light,
In the moon's embrace, soft and bright.
It flickers in the words unsaid,
In dreams where silent hopes are fed.

A spark that never fades away,
A promise of a brighter day.
In every tear, in every sigh,
The glimmer of love will never die.

Hold it close, a beacon in the vast,
A glimmer, pure and true,
For within it lies the essence of me and you.

Faded Glim

Space between hope and ache,
Fragile dreams that gently wake,
Yet time was swift, and fate unkind,
Leaving a hollow where love once twined.

Whispers lost in fleeting grace,
A tiny heartbeat's soft embrace,
Moments brief, they danced away,
Leaving a shadow in the day.

Echoes of a vanished bloom,
A tender loss, a silent plea,
A space where once a life could be.
A tender ache, a mournful heart.

Grief's quiet river, flowing slow,
Though dreams may drift and hopes may fade,
In every memory softly laid,
Lies a love that time can't part.

The Blue Butterfly

The quiet moments of the night,
When the world is still, and stars burn bright,
A mother's heart is working hard,
To give her all, never marred.

She let's go of dreams and bears the strain,
For every joy, for every pain.
Her sacrifices, both great and small,
Are signs of love, for one and all.

In every smile and every tear,
Her endless love is always near.
For all she gives, without a trace,
We honor her in each embrace.

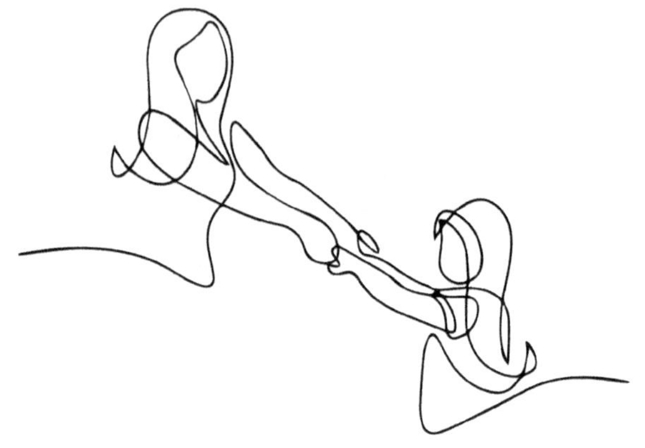

Unspoken Ties

In the quiet of the night, when shadows fall,
A sister's love is a comforting call.
When the world feels cold and dreams seem
far,
Her presence is a cynosure.

She's the keeper of your secrets, the balm for
every pain,
Through every loss and gain.
Her heart beats with a rhythm that echoes
your own.

In her embrace, your soul finds cures.
Memories shared, laughter, and tears,
A bond that deepens over the years.

In every trial, in every cheer,
A sister's love holds you near.
Though life may pull you far apart,
A sister's love is never too old.

Resurgence

Raindrops fell, and skies turned gray,
The world seemed lost in shadow's sway,
But just as gloom began to reign,
The sun broke through, dispelling the pain.

Golden rays on glistening leaves,
Nature's breath, a sigh it relieves,
The earth is fresh, the air is clear,
Hope returns, and hearts endear.

For every storm that clouds our way,
There's light ahead, a brighter day,
In every tear, a promise is made,
Sunshine follows, never delayed.

Silent Waters

In the twilight's grace,
I drift alone in a boat's embrace,
The world recedes, a distant shore,
With whispers of what once came before.

Water's calm, a mirror bright,
Reflecting stars, a silent night,
A sky so vast and midnight blue,
Where dreams and echoes wander through.

No compass guides, no charted course,
Just the steady pulse of the river's source,
The breeze that weaves through my hair,
A tender touch, a breath of air.

Each ripple tells a story spun,
Of battles lost, of races won,
But here in stillness, I remain,
A soul adrift, a quiet refrain.

The night will pass, the dawn will break,
Every care, every weight have known,

Carry it far, where the wild winds have blown.
In a drifting boat, alone in a world of my own.

Elegance of Forgiveness

In love's intricate waltz, we falter, we misstep,
Yet in the crucible of errors, resilience is
adept.
For love, though exalted, is tenderly flawed,
Balm of forgiveness, hearts are awed.
When words become daggers, and silence a
wall,
We are left to navigate through love's
wavering call.
Forgiveness, an art both rare and sublime,
Restores what was shattered by the passage of
time.
Forgiveness isn't submission, but valor
redefined,
It transcends the wounds, leaving anguish
behind.
To pardon is to liberate, to see with clear
sight,
The essence of love in its truest, pure light.
In this journey of hearts, where perfection
eludes,
We uncover grace in our shared interludes.

Forgiveness, a beacon in the tempestuous
night,
Illuminates love's path with unwavering light.
Being magnanimous, with spirits aligned,
For in forgiveness, love's depths are divined.
Trials may come, shadows may blend,
Forgiveness is the compass where true love
transcends.

The Quiet Strength

She wakes in the hush before dawn,
Bearing the weight of dreams and stakes,
Her hands, gentle, yet strong as steel,
Mend hearts, while her own wounds slowly
heal.

She is the keeper of whispered woes,
The one who stands when the wind blows,
With a heart that's wide and arms that
shelter,
A guardian, though life may welter.

In her eyes, the wisdom of years,
Swallows down her silent fears,
For the road she treads is long and steep,
Yet in her soul, secrets are kept.

She is the light in a stormy sea,
The one who always knows how to be,
Both the anchor and the sail,
guiding others when all else fails.

In the silence of the night, she ponders,

As the world around her gently slumbers,
Her spirit, fierce and bright,
Will rise again, will rise again..

Daughter, a tale untold,
Her worth far greater than gold,
A life lived for others, her heart so wide,
She carries the world with quiet pride.

Tangled Threads

A word misspoken, a glance misread,
Space between, where silence spreads,
Two hearts once close, now drift apart,
A simple misstep, yet miles apart.
The mind replays the scene so clear,
What was meant, what was heard, so near,
Yet tangled in the web of doubt,
What was truth now seems without.
A sigh a pause, and then a frown,
The weight of words now pulling down,
What was light and laughter before,
Now echoes softly, fading more.
But in the stillness, hope remains,
That time can heal and soothe the strains,
A simple word, a bridge rebuilt,
Can wash away the stain of guilt.
For in the end, it's often true,
That misunderstandings, though they brew,
Can be dissolved with gentle care,
And hearts can mend, if truth we share.

Tunnels

In the abyss where shadows brood,
A weary heart in solitude,
Traverses realms of endless night,
Yet glimpses faint, elusive light.
The tunnel winds with spectral grace,
A labyrinthine, somber space,
But in the distance, subtly shines,
A luminous, celestial sign.

The radiance swells with every stride,
A harbinger of dawn's divide,
Though the journey has been arduous and
stark,
The end reveals a guiding spark.
As darkness yields to nascent day,
Replaced by dawn's resplendent ray,
The light emerges, clear and true,
A testament to fortitude renewed.

Infinite

In the depths where feelings flow,
There lies a love that's deep and slow,
Unspoken, yet it resonates,
A force that time and space deflates.

Found in moments, tender, still,
In every glance, in every thrill,
A bond that no mere words can keep,
A love that's vast, eternal, and steep.

Roots extend through joy and pain,
Through summer's warmth and winter's rain,
A current flowing, pure and true,
That binds two hearts in every hue.

So deep, it surpasses earth and sky,
A timeless truth that won't deny,
A love that in the soul does seep,
An ocean wide, a love so deep.

In Her

I love her, the one who stumbles,
Whose laughter occasionally cracks mid-air,
Whose tears fall silently in the quiet corners,
Where no one sees, but I am there.

I love her in the chaos spinning,
When doubts dance ferociously beneath her
skin,
When she feels like breaking, crumbling,
I gather her, and tuck her in.

I love her scars, the tales they whisper,
Of nights she thought she couldn't stand,
Of days when shadows stretched endlessly,
Yet still she rose with trembling hands.

I love her voice, though sometimes shaking,
Though silenced by the world's unforgiving
demands,
For in its whispers, there is power,
A song that only she comprehends.

I love her flaws, her edges jagged,

The cracks that let the light slip through,
For in her messy, human essence,
she shines more brightly, deeply true.

I love her most in the ugly moments,
When the mirror reflects a tired face,
For even then, beneath the surface,
There's a quiet strength, a sacred grace.

So here I stand, arms open wide,
Embracing all that she has been,
For every fall, and every triumph, I love her
still.

Harmonies

In every breath, a symphony hums,
A rhythm where the silence beats,
A dance of shadows, light, and time,
Where every note becomes a symphony.

The strings that ache, the horns that soar,
Unlocking worlds behind shut doors,
A language only hearts can speak,
Where words fall short and whispers peak.

The bass, a pulse beneath our skin,
The keys unlock what's concealed within,
Each crescendo, a leap of faith,
Each rest, a moment wrapped in grace.

A symphony of life unfolds,
In melodies both brave and bold,
And though the song may rise and fall,
Its echo lingers, resonates through us all.

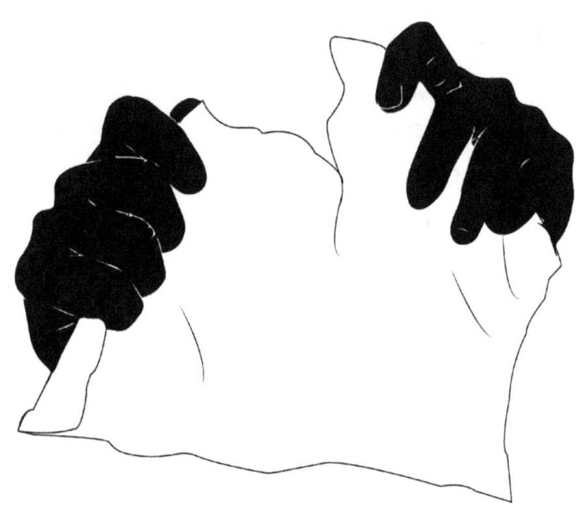

Cutting the Chord

A string that's fraying, and notes no longer
resonate,
Cut the ties that once bound,
Releasing whispers I no longer hear.

A tune that time has weathered,
A symphony now lost in twilight,
The melody that tied our hearts,
Unravels in the fading musk.

Each severed strand holds a memory,
Each fragment holds a piece of us,
Yet as I cut through past's thin threads,
To a quiet strength, emerges.

The silence grows where music lingered,
A space to breathe, to find rebirth,
In cutting the chord of old affection,
I open doors to paths unviewed.

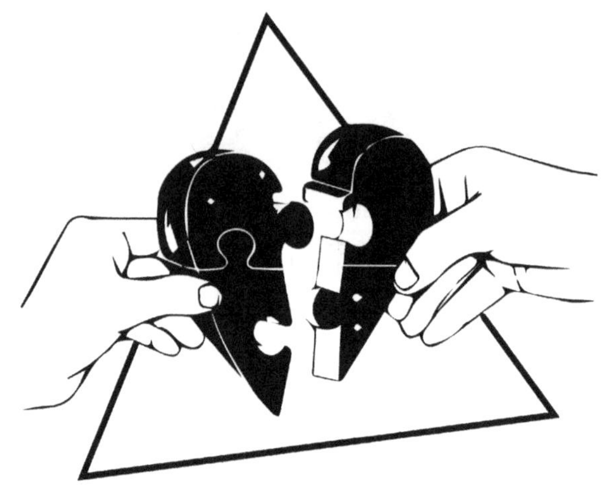

Perfectly Odd Together

We are like mismatched socks and cereal for
dinner,
A little bit crazy, and full of fun,
My partner in all things quirky,
The moon to my sun.

We laugh at jokes that make no sense,
And dance in our pajamas, too,
In a world that's often so serious,
I'm glad we found us..

Your quirks are my favorite playlist,
Your oddities make me smile wide,
In our own strange way,
Together, we take life in our stride.

So here's to our whimsical journey,
With its twists and joy,
Forever my oddball soulmate,
You're the best kind of crazy for me.

Morning Dew

Dayspring, dainty and warm,
Touch the green April orchids gently.

Through dark leaves, rain pools reflect,
Silver fragments of the sky's expanse.

Glory flashes briefly through a western
window's fire opal,
Layered in smoky richness,

As dusk turns to purple plums.
Across the serene azure calm, the butter
moon drifts,

Blossoming over the still lake,
Embracing the blue depths in a hushed
whisper.

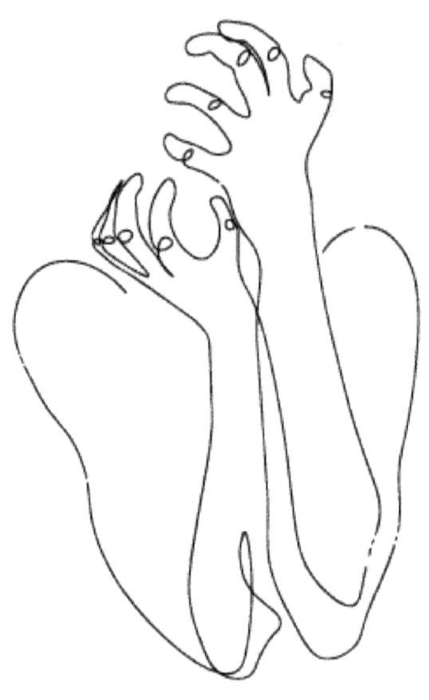

Hope to Despair

There's a moment out of reach,
A place we cannot trace,
Where fate is sealed for every soul,
In triumph or disgrace.

An invisible divide we miss,
That touches all we know,
A hidden line between heaven's grace
And wrath's unyielding blow.

Why this enigmatic thread
That shapes our mortal course.
Beyond which even gods have pledged
The soul to endless force.

How long will sin's grip hold me tight?
How long will grace extend?
Where does hope's journey end,
And where does despair begin.

In Silent Harmony

Without a word, without a sign,
In the hush where hearts entwine,
I love you for the silent art,
That stirs the soul and heals the heart.

In the stillness, our spirits meet,
Where words dissolve, and hearts retreat.
Not just for who you are revealed,
But for the self in you concealed.

You are the canvas, pure and bright,
Where I paint my soul's delight.
In our quiet, unspoken space,
I find myself, and found my place.

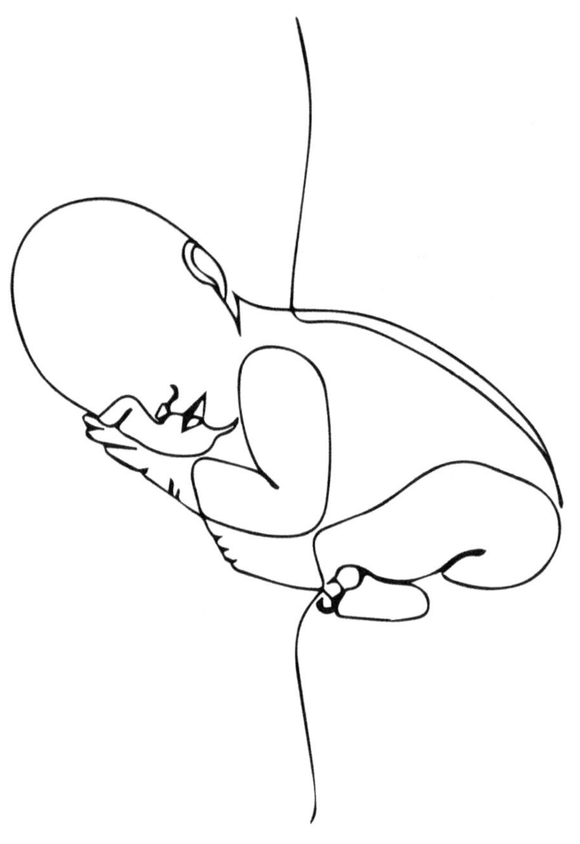

Unborn

All my dreams of nurturing you,
As a balanced soul, now drift away,
For you chose to end before you grew.

You took from me the chance to raise
A caring heart, a future bright,
A child who would learn to value love
To understand a woman's light.

Where men see mere pleasure's prize,
Yearned to shape you, guide your way,
To appreciate the care and warmth
That fuels us from day to day.

You would have known the heart that yearns
For freedom yet embraces ties,
And seen the smile through morning's chore,
A reflection of love in her eyes.

Ways of Nature

The teak tree's regal stance in spring,
A jade clad dance in my garden,
New green shoots like armor gleamed,
They brightly beamed, in sunlight's grace.

As days unfolded, gold cones spun,
Laced with diamonds, each one a sun,
But autumn's whisper, winter's breath,
Turned the shimmer cold and bereft.

Green turned to brittle brown and stark,
A mirror of youth's fleeting spark,
Man, in his prime, so vibrant, bold,
With time's passage, loses his hold.

Unlike the tree that will revive,
In spring's embrace, anew and alive,
Man cannot turn back the fleeting years,
A truth reflected in nature's tears.

Yearning for a Heartbeat

I yearn, in the quiet of my dreams,
My heart burns for a love so deep,
To hold a child, a precious gift,
And feel my soul in tender lift.

I ache for moments pure and true,
For sleepless nights and mornings new,
A tiny heartbeat, soft and warm,
A life to cradle, to keep from harm.

In the echoes of my deepest wishes,
I envision small hands, gentle kisses,
A future filled with joy and care,
A bond of love beyond compare.

I long for the embrace of this sweet fate,
To be a mother, to celebrate,
A dream of life and love entwined,
A hope that stirs within my mind.

* 9 7 8 9 3 6 3 3 0 7 4 1 4 *